yoga Healing love

Yoga Healing Love

Poem Blessings for a Peaceful Mind and Happy Heart

TAMMY STONE TAKAHASHI

2021

GOLDEN DRAGONFLY PRESS

FIRST PRINT EDITION, May 2021
FIRST EBOOK EDITION, May 2021

ISBN–13: 978-1-7330099-6-6
Library of Congress Control Number: 2021937022

Printed on acid-free paper supplied by a
Forest Stewardship Council-certified provider.
First published in the United States of America
by Golden Dragonfly Press, 2021.

www.goldendragonflypress.com

@tammystonetakahashi
www.tammystone.weebly.com

for my teachers, Beatrix and Pancho,

for showing me the path of love, with love, for love.

Contents

Acknowledgments

This book comes out of a community of love and respect, not only for the principles of yoga but also the collective drive for peace, and a happy, thriving humanity. I'm so grateful to my teachers, Pancho and Beatrix, for introducing me to the spiritual path of yoga, and for being such a tremendous support to me over the years, in more ways than I can count. I'd like to thank George Kaltsounakis who, in addition to being a true and lifetime friend, has lent his brilliant editing skills to this collection. Huge bows of gratitude to Catherine L. Schweig for her constant and loving encouragement of my work over the years, and for publishing the poem "I Choose Love", which appears in this collection, on her beautiful blog, *Journey of the Heart*. All my humble gratitude to Alice Maldonado Gallardo, of Golden Dragonfly Press, for her unwavering encouragement and tireless efforts in transforming, like alchemy, the words inside this collection into this book, which I hope will reach anyone who might benefit from it. Thank you to all the beautiful yogis, yoginis and humans I've had the great fortune of growing alongside all these years, including Holger Meinberg, who never tires of holding my hand, and my husband, Takeshi Takahashi, who helps me grow and reflect on how to offer of myself to this world every single day.

Introduction

*"The rhythm of the body, the melody of the mind
and the harmony of the soul create the symphony of life."*

—B.K.S. IYENGAR

In my personal experience, this symphony of life beautifully pointed to by one of yoga's great masters, B.K.S. Iyengar, is not always easy or natural to awaken to. Everything from our ordinary and intimate daily routines to our experience of the greater world out there can be riddled with sources of tension, stress, conflict and fear, despite our greatest hopes for peace and harmony. I remember feeling acutely aware of–and surprised by–just how unbalanced I felt when I first stepped onto a yoga mat what seems like a lifetime ago–many, many moons before now, in any case!

I'd actually been introduced to yoga sometime before then, during a very hectic time: I was pursuing my PhD (I was studying the role observation plays in our daily lives, a potentially yogic topic, though I can't say I was aware of this), and I'd also begun working a full-time job in the world of film festivals and programming. I loved these pursuits, as well as living in the bustling, multicultural city of Toronto, but I also found myself feeling drained a lot of the time. It was a physical sense of fatigue (I struggled with headaches and insomnia) and, even more so, an emotional and a psychological one. It was also, looking back, very much a spiritual exhaustion, though I would have been very hesitant about using that word at the time.

I can remember two distinct events from that time that stand out as beacons of my journey to come. One was a friend of mine giving me a VHS tape of a 20-minute power yoga video. He was purging his closet and tossed the tape to me saying, "I thought you might like this." We'd never talked about yoga, much less broached the idea of me engaging in a practice of any sort, but I welcomed the thoughtful gift and gave it a try later that night. I stumbled, fell, cursed, and simply couldn't believe how hard it was to achieve balance in the body I'd been carrying around with me my whole life in a fairly functional way. How fragile we are, I marveled when I calmed down, how easy to topple over, and how dependent on our customary, conditioned ways of standing, let alone thinking and being. I did this tape, and found a couple of others, and continued to do these on and off for a few months, before my life turned upside down.

Around this time, I also met with another fascinating experience when my ex-boyfriend, with whom I was still close, told me that he'd been encouraged to try Reiki and that he thought I'd really enjoy it. I listened, and booked an appointment. Before the treatment even began, I loved being in the presence of this practitioner. She told me she could see that I was utterly depleted. She asked me if I drank coffee and when I said I did, she said I really didn't need to, that my energy was extremely bright and powerful and that coffee would only step in the way of that, despite my current state of feeling emptied out.

And was I ever emptied out! I had just turned 35, an age of extreme significance to me. When I was around 20, a group of friends and I had sat around trying to figure out what each of our "soul ages" were—the ages we felt we had always been deep down. We decided mine was 35, and I always imagined this would be a time I'd feel satisfied and deeply fulfilled in all areas of my life. This was not how things were turning out, though. I had a decent job that was slowly starting to feel like a mess, in no small part due to my confusion over ending up in a career I loved but had never truly chosen. Despite having beautiful and close friendships, I was in a string of unhealthy relationships with unavailable men, and there was an overwhelming feeling that I was missing the mark somehow, that my life purpose was eluding me.

Seeds had been planted, though, like the ones I've just described, and also during the long periods of time I'd spent traveling and living in Southeast Asia (I lived there for a year in 2001, and went back many times after that). When I finally lost my job, I knew the time had come to put a decisive halt to my current life. I got rid of my apartment, dumped my things in my parents' basement (thank you mom and dad!) and booked a one-way flight to Thailand. And here is where my journey with yoga and Reiki began in earnest, like they had been waiting for me all along.

Studying with brilliant, wonderful teachers Pancho and Beatrix at the Nong Khai Yoga, Reiki, Therapy and Astrology Center in Thailand, I delved not only into the physical, or *asana* portion of yoga, but the philosophical and spiritual aspects of it as well. They taught me with such profundity that yoga is not just a series of physical movements, but a true path to awakening that can take many forms. I immediately gravitated toward this approach that integrated breath and movement with the notions of striving for balance and union within myself and with the greater universe. I realized that I didn't need to conceptually understand everything about how the cosmos operated, but that I could trust good and true teachers, and also have faith in my own ability to let go of beliefs and conditioned patterns of thinking, and just give myself over to the process of becoming. It felt like being an infant taking her first steps, yet I was armed with an adult's awareness that these steps were going to guide me to a more holistic way of feeling and being in the world. Having faith, in others, in the process of healing, and in the universe itself, I discovered, brings untold blessings in as many forms as we'll allow ourselves to experience.

I've written the poems in this book in part as a gift of gratitude to my teachers and to the ancient wisdom of yoga itself for the innumerable gifts it has brought to my life as I've slowly learned to open my psyche and allow for healing to occur, and for love to pour in and to flood out. I've watched with wonder as my poetry has transformed along with my awareness that writing is an intrinsic part of my spiritual path. It is my great wish to offer the poems in this collection as a reflection of my love for and appreciation of this path, and as a contribution to the vast array of beautiful poetry in the world celebrating the mystical and magical union that exists between all people, all sentient beings, and between all beings and the bountiful nature from which we arise, and of which we are an inextricable part. As such, these poems, while an enriching companion for any student of the path of yoga seeking empowerment, embodiment and divine union, are meant for everyone: I believe that yoga lives inside all of us, ready to revitalize the spirit, and can be aided by the unique power of poetry to move us beyond the realm of the intellect, where the heart resides.

The hand that writes poems, as I see it, is an extension of a yearning, seeking, hopeful and loving heart seeking to express the ineffable and inexpressible, as best as it can. Poetry has been an important and sacred part of my yogic and spiritual path, and it delights me to bring poetry and yoga together into a collection like this that is at its heart designed for self-reflection, self-awareness and self-care with an eye toward transcending the self and moving toward unity—with all beings, and the source of all things. Ultimately, our journey of enlightenment begins with the "I" and moves toward the "we". This is what yoga is all about!

The book begins with seven poems for each of the main *chakras*, or "wheels" in Sanskrit. In yoga, Reiki, meditation and the ancient Indian healing system of Ayurveda, the chakras are known as energy centres located at different points in the body where matter meets with different bodies or levels of consciousness, with the seven major chakras found along the body's central meridian, from the very base of the spine to the crown of the head. These seven chakras–from the bottom up *muladhara* (root chakra), *svadisthana* (navel chakra), *manipura* (solar plexus chakra), *anahata* (heart chakra), *vishuddhi* (throat chakra), *ajna* (third eye chakra) and *sahasrara* (crown chakra)–relate to or correspond with different physical, mental, emotional and spiritual aspects of being. My intention with these poems is to call attention to the special qualities of each chakra in a way that can inspire awareness in readers wishing to spend time engaging with these energy centers in a deeper way.

The rest of the book consists of 108 poem-blessings that are also designed to nourish, nurture and complement a yoga or meditative practice on and off the mat. They can be read during *savasana* (corpse pose, or the resting position at the end of a yoga practice), during the mindful resting portion at the end of a yoga asana practice when the body is ripe for absorption and integration, or prior to meditation, to simply set a peaceful and in-spired tone for the day or for sleep. They can be read in any order, at any time of day; my intention is for each poem to serve as a ray of sunshine, or perhaps as a moonbeam, helping you open the doors to your beautiful inner wisdom. Every poem in the book is written in the first person, so that whether you are reading the poems quietly in your head, or out loud, they can have the effect of a personal meditation and affirmation. This is not meant to cocoon the reader within the shell of the "I", but rather, to further connect each "I"–each person reading them–to the greater One, in which we are all a beautiful part. There is so much we can accomplish together, in unity.

The poems also offer anyone looking to explore different layers of meaning in their lives a means of tapping into their sense of gratitude, mindfulness and awakening.

108 is a deeply spiritual and mystical number, known to represent spiritual completion in various Eastern religions and practices. There are thought to be 108 forms of meditation, and in Buddhism, there are 108 earthly desires and obstacles to the path of enlightenment, so that when you use *mala* or prayer beads, which have 108 beads, and pass your fingers over each bead, you are purifying by removing an obstacle to your awakening. In the yogic system, there are 108 *nadis*, or energy lines that converge at the heart chakra, the center of our loving existence, where our true intelligence resides.

In Hinduism, each of the deities has 108 names, which inspired the naming of the poems in this book. Lord Shiva, as the deity Yogeshwar, is the Lord of Yoga, reigning over all aspects of the practice, including physical, mental, emotional and spiritual. He represents the energy, or *prana*, which cannot die and which ignites all beings, and rules the realms of meditation, the ascension of power, and transcendence. Shiva, then, is the guru of yoga, through which we come in touch with the guru within, much like how in Buddhism, we are seeking to understand and embrace our own inner Buddha nature. I would love to imagine that as you read the poems of this book, you might allow yourself the luxury of lingering over the beautiful names of Shiva, each of which is already a beautiful little prayer to delight the tongue, ear and heart, as you absorb this deity's innumerable cherished qualities as parts of your own nature. I've added an Appendix to the end of the book listing the 108 attributes of Shiva so that you can even more powerfully come into connection with these divine, yet human qualities.

The magic of 108 goes on! 108 is also the number you multiply the Sun's diameter by to get the average distance between the Sun and the Earth; and the average distance between the Earth and the Moon is 108 times greater than the Moon's diameter—two little kernels of knowledge I absolutely love! The Sun and Moon are deeply significant in the yoga practice—the "ha" in *hatha* yoga means Sun in Sanskrit and "tha" means Moon. These respectively represent the yang and the yin, the opposition and ultimate union of masculine and feminine, power and gentility, action and intuition, grounded and spiritual pursuits.

In the yogic tradition, it is widely understood that every being strives to find a balance between these opposing energies. We work, through our yoga practice, to embrace the masculine and female energies within us, and transcend our notions of conflict and duality to come to a place of balance, oneness and union with whatever conception of the divine is meaningful, useful and productive for us. We do not achieve this union by ignoring our history, or any of the obstacles we will inevitably confront on our path. Instead, we learn to be mindful and aware of what makes us who we are, as we work to smooth the edges of our existence, face our challenges with love and equanimity, and find peace with and acceptance for the beautiful and unique beings that we are. With peace and acceptance comes the possibility for a true, grounded, unconditional love, and a compassion that can bring us infinite happiness and do no less than save the world.

May the poems and blessings in this book—and the three bonus stories for children and the children within—bring joy and be of benefit to you in your journey of discovery and growth.

Blessings!

With love,

Tammy

CHAKRA POEMS

"When you touch the celestial in your heart, you will realize that the beauty of your soul is so pure, so vast and so devastating that you have no option but to merge with it. You have no option but to feel the rhythm of the universe in the rhythm of your heart."

—AMIT RAY

Muladhara
(Root Chakra)

I am here

Here you are.
I hear it in the rustling wind
and feel it in the grass under my feet.
I am here.
I am resting here
in the knowledge that my existence
is a divine and holy act.
Yes, here you are.
I am here,
and I belong here.
I am one with our blessed universe.
I feel this sacred connection
and I bow to all creatures and beings.
I stand on the rich and nurturing ground
and feel it pulsing beneath me,
from the soles of my feet
to the crown of my head, and beyond.
Proud, I am a child of Earth
and I stand tall, fierce and brave.
Like a tree, I root deep into the ground,
and like a mountain, I rise to my power.
I stand blissfully in the seat of my own being,

and feel safe within Earth's womb.
All that I have, I give and share,
as I see, hear, touch and smell
the wondrous offerings of our planet,
and know I would do anything to protect Her,
as She protects me.
May I always be protected.
May I always feel safe.
May I always honor our perfect existence,
and my divine right to exist,
to be exactly and purely who I am.

Svadisthana
(Navel Chakra)

I feel

I am here and I feel I am here.
I take a glorious, deep breath
and walk from land to shore,
and wade into the deep waters.
I smile and close my eyes
as the waves caress my skin,
the salty air swelling around me
as the ocean takes me into her
vast and loving embrace.
I marvel at the totality of creation
and bow before all
that has given me life.
I acknowledge, too,
that my divine existence
is a perfect act of creation,
and that creating is my birthright.
I can feel it deep in my bones,
and in the water that flows
through my earthly body.
My feelings are as natural and cyclical
as the Sun's rise and fall,
the Moon's wax and wane.

I notice the feelings that guide me
as the Moon guides the way of the ocean.
I honor my feelings
and I awaken to myself
in relationship
to the feelings in me
and the feelings in you,
so that we illumine each other
in the safety and bliss
of our mutual love and
divine understanding.
May I listen to the beautiful call
of my emotions
and may I stay true
to my divine right to create and feel.
May we grow in relationship,
together.

Manipura
(Solar Plexus Chakra)

I am

I have come into this world,
alive, powerful and free: I am.
I am, and I know that I am.
I blaze my way forward,
now sure of my path.
Blessed with a strong vision
of where I want to go,
I make my way there,
calm, certain and bold.
The bright golden Sun
lends a deep clarity to the day.
I can see what I need to do.
I have felt my way here
and I am learning what
I need to know.
The Sun blazes within me too,
radiating from my core
to the outer reaches
of my body, mind and spirit.
I am filled with the joy
my life's mission brings
as I gather strength from

the Earth below,
and from the deepest parts
flowing within me,
and I begin
from my strong and stable center
as I strive for even greater
clarity, intellect and wisdom.
And so I go,
climbing ever upward
on a foundation of Love,
the wisdom of the Sun my guide.
May I always strive for clarity.
May I always rest in wisdom.
May I always recognize
the honor and beauty of *I am*.

Anahata
(Heart Chakra)

I love

I love. Oh, but I love.
Arching back, I raise my chest to the sky,
and I can feel our enchanted world
echoing in the chambers of my heart.
I have walked a million miles
and tasted all the joys and sorrows.
I have danced with pain
and crumbled from desiring so much,
all so that I could arrive at this,
a better understanding of love,
to live with love, *to be love*.
It is love that heals me,
taking heartache into its gentle fold,
soothing and nurturing it
so that I may open enough
to feel everyone's suffering
and remain in communion with all beings
in our long and beautiful,
shared experience.
How alive I feel in our shared heartbeat,
this sacred awakened consciousness!
Oh, how we rise together!

I feel you within me,
and I within you.
I feel the rhythms of the Earth
beating in each and every one of us.
I hold your hand as you hold mine
as we feel love in the deepest
reaches of the compassionate heart,
transcending this one moment
and dwelling in all of eternity together.
May I always strive to honor
the empathy and joy within me.
May love be my greatest teacher.
May I allow universal love to heal me.
May we live with love and as love,
always.

Vishuddhi
(Throat Chakra)

I sing

I sing.
I belong to the realm
of pure expression, and I sing.
I sing nothing less than
the exquisite song of our existence.
It is an ancient, timeless song
I have discovered within me,
dark and haunting,
but also suffused with the light
of divine wisdom.
My senses unite in this sublime song
and it is my greatest wish
to give the gift of voice
to the longings of my heart,
the thrumming energy
pouring through my being.
I sing to you
so that I may hear your song
as I tune myself to the universal chord
in a melody meant for us,
and unleash untold powers within.
As we sing united,

we join a mystical and sacred circle
where there are no bounds,
only infinite possibility
and the deep wisdom of the ages.
Even on cold dark nights, I sing.
Even when loneliness reigns, I sing.
I sing, louder and louder still,
until I start to know the song of my self.
May I honor my right to express my heart.
May I always trust the wisdom of my Truth.
May I forever exist in communion
with all beings, and the Divine.
May we always unite in voice together.

Ajna

(Third Eye Chakra)

'I see'

I see.
Like the great seers before me,
I see and I embrace my desire
to live with vision.
From the sanctity of my physical body,
I work to lift the veil
so I can see what lies
beyond the world of the senses.
Oh, but the stars!
It is here that I long to dwell.
It is here that I find myself dancing.
The light is shining and beautiful.
The Sun and Moon converge,
the celestial and lunar energies
come into harmony and spark
their healing fire between
my searching eyes,
and guide my vision within,
uniting me with the greater cosmic story.
It is an inner knowing,
a deep, pure and true awareness
of who I am in body and spirit,

of where I've been,
of how things are
and how they need to be.
With great fluidity
I navigate untold paths,
leading to greater illumination.
I weave through space and time,
from the ocean floors to bluest skies
finding connection and light in all.
May I always trust my inner light.
May I always be guided from within.
May I always aspire for the highest good,
the greatest depths of being, and infinite wisdom.

Sahasrara
(Crown Chakra)

'I am One'

I am One.
From the many selves
I have been on this journey of life,
I merge into the sublime awareness
of unity, and aspire to remain
in Oneness.
I have felt the Earth under my feet,
I have sat, feeling the contours of my body,
knowing the sensations of the Sun on my skin,
the flow of the tides sweeping through me,
the fire in my belly, the aching, the longing,
the loving of my heart.
I have sung and danced with the angels
and found perfect stillness in my being.
I have listened deep within myself
and heard all the ancient stories.
It has all come to this,
awash in the brightest light,
bathing in the golden splendor of Union.
The movements are infinite, celestial and pure.
This is a new consciousness
free of division,

devoid of a *you* and a *me*.
Our source comes forth
in warm greeting,
and I am finally ready
to enter through this divine gateway.
May I always aspire
for the dissolution of my ego.
May I always aspire
to fold my consciousness into the Divine.
May I always live in the light
of my spirituality, and my highest self.
May I always trust
in the beauty, splendor and majesty
of the Universal One.

108

BLESSING POEMS

*"The more dedicated you are, the more open you become.
The more open you remain, the more love you experience.
The more love you give, the more grace you receive.
It is this grace that will bring You to the goal."*

— MĀTĀ AMRITĀNANDAMAYĪ DEVĪ AMMA

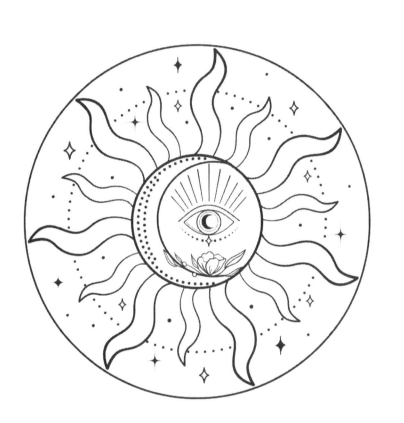

The poems on the pages that follow are dedicated to Lord Shiva, Guru of Yoga, who like each of the Hindu deities has 108 names. I've chosen to use the blessing form of the name instead of the name alone for the title of each poem. For example, the first of Lord Shiva's names is "Shiva," and the blessing form of the name used below is "Om Shivaya Namah." Om is a mystic symbol, and the most sacred sound and mantra in Hinduism and Tibetan Buddhism. It is pure being, and divine presence; it is all sounds in one sound. "Namah" means "to bow" or "to prostrate before." The common translation of "Om Namah Shivaya" or here, "Om Shivaya Namah" is "O salutations to the auspicious one" or "universal consciousness is one." We don't need to get caught up in the exact translation! Rather, we can imagine that as we read each poem title, we are bowing to one of the 108 aspects of Shiva, or the divine nature inside all of us. I encourage you to linger over these poem title/mantras, and even read them out loud, as there is a genuinely beautiful, soothing quality and healing effect inherent in absorbing these words, and hearing the lulling, melodic sounds they make when softly spoken by the human voice.

I've also numbered all the poems, so that the number becomes a part of the poem's title. You can imagine it as though you are using your *mala*, or prayer beads. As you count each bead, you are immersing yourself in a ritual of purification, removing obstacles one by one on the path to joy.

1. Om Shivaya Namah

Muladhara: Thank you for my will to be ALIVE.

Svadisthana: Thank you for my feeling of connectedness to ALL.

Manipura: Thank you for my determination to BE.

Anahata: Thank you for my kind, soft heart, open to LOVE.

Vishuddhi: Thank you for my desire to create and receive WISDOM.

Ajna: Thank you for your guidance, and my INNER SIGHT.

Sahasrara: Thank you for helping me merge with the DIVINE.

2. Om Maheshwaraya Namah

May I expand with each in-breath
as the flower awakens in the Sun.
May I release with each out-breath,
as the flower sighs and folds in
when the day gives way to dusk.

3. Om Shambhave Namah

The Sun's gifts are boundless;
may my heart be boundless, too.
There is nothing that doesn't glow
in the light's brilliant perfection.
May my spirit arrive at the light
and be courageous enough
to live there, to dance there,
to grow and to thrive there.
May I with each breath honor
the body of light that I am,
that I have always been,
that I will always and ever be.

4. Om Pinakine Namah

I am alive.
I brim with aliveness!
I love the breath I breathe.
I love the body I breathe in.
I love the world I breathe into.
I love all the beings
that inhabit our Earth
and breathe as we all breathe,
as fish glide in the water,
as clouds disperse in the air,
as trees drink from the ground.
May I always breathe love in.
May I always breathe love out.
May I always notice every breath.
May I bow to my life with gratitude.

5. Om Shashishekharaya Namah

The morning dawns bright,
as a golden ball
of life-sustaining fire
breathes to sustain us.
May I rise with the Sun.
May I rise in my thoughts
and in my prayers.
May I rise through my words
and in my every action.
May I always be rising,
without any thought of limit,
pure, simple, true and free.

6. Om Vamadevaya Namah

Today, I will strive
to be like a leaf,
not thinking, doubting
or wondering.
Like a beautiful leaf,
I will open
to the light of this day,
and rest in a state
of complete openness.
May I remain open
to receiving the light
and depth of love's love,
like a leaf,
which has never once
thought to hide
from life's storms,
instead,
allowing the ravages
of wind and rain
as it does the bright healing
of Sun,
knowing that the rain, too,
nourishes,
and that the wind carries
messages of comfort
that together with Sun,
create the alchemy
of this precious life.

7. Om Virupakshaya Namah

In serene stillness
I receive the universe
in my field of consciousness.
It is vast, pure and light
larger than I can imagine,
limitless and expansive
as it forms a bubble
of protection around me,
in shimmering, golden white.
I lie awake, restful,
so that I can hear my breath
rise and fall to the rhythm
of the world's heart beating,
and feel that I am part
of the grand universal song,
the song of Om,
the song of One,
the song of home,
our one true song.

8. Om Kapardine Namah

I am more than my pain and sadness.
I am more than my joy and triumphs.
I am more than my stories and my history.
I am more than what ails me
and more than what gives me pride.
I am more than what I can see, touch and feel,
and more than the thoughts in my mind.
I am so much more than these parts of me.
In the spectral light of all that exists,
and shielded by an unguarded purity,
I tap into the endlessness of what lies within,
and come to see with the greatest wonder,
not that I am this, or I am that,
but just this: that I Am.
I am. I am. I am.

9. Om Nilalohiytaya Namah

May I always see the world
just as it is,
and may I always see myself
just as I am,
perfect in my beautiful
and delicate humanity,
perfect in struggle,
perfect in my being
in this body, in this moment.
As I strive for union,
a feeling of wholeness in the One,
may I also find myself at peace
with what is fractured
and what is wounded,
and may I recognize this
as the gift of my birth,
as I begin each day
knowing it is the very beginning
of the long and dazzling
journey home.

10. Om Shankaraya Namah

Just for today,
I will look at my body
and see a wellspring of vitality,
and appreciate the magnificence
of a sacred being
working in soft gentle harmony
so that I may be.

Just for today,
I will offer thanks
to the parts of my body
that I can see,
for moving with me
through this vast and trying life
unbound in the *I*, and in the *we*.

Just for today,
I will be thankful
for the parts of my body
that I cannot see,
for everything they do
beyond the cloak of visibility
so that I may be all of me.

Just for today,
I will thank myself
for choosing to be with my body,
and immersing with such great courage
in the depths of what pains me,
so that I may release it,
and rest in the transcendence of the free.

11. Om Shulapanaye Namah

Today's a new day,
like none the world has seen.
There's a new Sun to bathe in,
a new ground to walk on,
new air to take in.
It's a new day already filling up
with the colors and sounds
of a world falling in love
with itself all over again,
a world made of love
and designed for loving.
May I choose love
and nothing but love
on this brilliant new day,
and on every new day
that greets me.

12. Om Khatvangine Namah

It's time.
It's time to find
the wildness
I bear within,
my deepdown jewels,
my seeds of freedom

The wild
that protects
my long-held desires
that need not
be suppressed,
that will not be oppressed

The wild
born of wisdom
that knows where I have strayed,
where I've lost
the secret pathways
from my heart to the world

To be
the wild one
I've always been, rooted and rising,
fiery in knowing
of my ancient longing
for the dawn of our tomorrow as One.

13. Om Vishnuvallabhaya Namah

Take me to the Sun,
and I will show you
how much I am trying
to bring the light in me
into the light of the world.

Show me the Moon,
and I will sit with you
so we can feel together
the swell of our hearts
in the tender spaces within.

Remind me of the ground
and I will bow in gratitude
for this reminder of home
underneath my feet,
which connects me to you.

Bring me to my breath,
and the air around us
that is filled with all joys
and the possibility
of movement, and ecstasy.

Sit with me by what is holy,
and watch how spirit arises.
Stand with me by a mountain
and know the trembling power
of our fierce hope rising.

14. Om Shipivishtaya Namah

How do we heal
a world that is burning?
We douse the fire with love.

How do we heal
a people divided?
We face what divides us with love.

How do we heal
generations of trauma?
We tend to that trauma with love.

How do we heal
our pained and wounded bodies?
We listen to those bodies with love.

We don't run away,
or fill our heads with stories,
or look for ways to shame, and blame.

We listen, with no judgment.
We listen, with curiosity and compassion.
We listen, so that we may hear.

May we hear, so that we may know.
May we share, so that we may grow,
and fill the space between us with love.

15. Om Ambikanathaya Namah

The tree,
in the still clarity of the moment,
offers everything of herself,
holds nothing inside,
and receives,
as it freely gives.
Like the tree,
may I allow myself
to receive the bounty
that is always
available to me.
May I understand
that giving and receiving
are like the in-breath
and the out-breath,
serving each other,
serving the greatness
of shared being.

16. Om Shrikanthaya Namah

I sit on soft ground.
Humming and alive,
it holds my mind gingerly,
as I reach for the
cloudless
sky,

Knowing,

That neither the Sun,
nor the Moon
asks of the other.
There is a sharing
of the vast skies,
a time for each,
and ends bleed into beginnings.
May we, too,
like the Sun and Moon,
hold the other dear,
shine as only we can,
and dance through
all this grace.

17. Om Bhaktavatsalaya Namah

I sit low so that I can feel
my origins seep into me,
my life's blood,
from you, the great Mother.
I gaze upward,
in each of the directions
to find more of the forces
that create and sustain me,
and feel myself as I am,
a being between sea and sky,
where ocean meets land,
and I am a whirl of life,
fire and air whipping through me,
water pulsing through me,
earth my most solid friend.
I take root in the elements,
and allow myself to move,
and feel these movements
taking me on the longest
and farthest journey I've known.
Back here. To me. To home.
May I always rejoice
in the sacred, homeward dance.

18. Om Bhavaya Namah

Each day, may I wake up to joy.
Every night, may I let go of my sadness.
Each day, may I learn one new thing.
Every night, may I rest body, mind and soul.
Each day, may my spirit rise with the Sun.
Every night, may I reflect deeply with the Moon.
Each day, may I begin with new eyes.
Every night, may I give thanks for all I've seen.

19. Om Sharvaya Namah

In every dream,
we come together
in longing, hope
and aspiration.
May I know love.
May I know love.
May I finally,
finally know love.

For love,
without being a language,
breathes music into words
and symphonies into speech.
Love will never let us forget love.
Her existence is woven into our own
the way the ocean lives in a pearl,
and all we ever had to do
was remember.

20. Om Trilokeshaya Namah

I sit in quiet repose
allowing the silence to fill me.
I breathe in and the outer world expands.
I breathe out and my inner being swells.
May everyone be surrounded,
always, by love's expansive breath,
that whispers into the heart, *I am...*

I am a new morning rising, a day begun.
I am the womb of time, protector of hope.
I am night falling, a kiss on your forehead.
I am the desert sand, gleaming like gold.
I am the cold of dawn, and the heat of day.
I am a seed below ground, ready to grow.
I am a little bird, bringing peace from afar.
I am the sacred wind, carrying all ancient wisdom.
I am the Sun you see, and the suns beyond time.
I am grandfather tree, echoing your name.
I am mother Moon, a light upon shadows.
I am solid Earth, under your feet.
I am oceans vast, deep, blue.
I am, for you.
I am.

21. Om Shitikanthaya Namah

Silence, my witness
I come to you softly

Because it is now
the time for seeing.

I shake loose what
has kept me from you,

I sit down on a ground
that holds me with

Her warmth. She wants
me here. I close my eyes.

I don't know what to do.
But I cannot be anywhere

Else. The ground, pure
force, is telling me, *stay*.

This is not about knowing.
It is about surrender, and

My firm desire to be here.
To peer into the silence

And find what shines bright.
The tears tell me I've arrived

Where I'm needed. And so I do:
silence, may I surrender to you.

22. Om Shivapriyaya Namah

A leaf up close
is a world
of cosmic creation

Lines etched
on nature's green
untouched by our worry.

To climb
this little leaf
and choose a direction,

As I would
a magic carpet
bound for the end of time,

And I can, and do.
With each breath, may I climb,
and witness the pathways, and destination.

23. Om Ugraya Namah

Resting, I bow before the Moon,
taking comfort in her glowing light.
Gently, I stretch my limbs,
expanding under the Moon's wisdom.
With love, I take your hand,
honoring our shared connection
under all the Moon's phases,
knowing there is no true expansion,
unless we are all growing together,
knowing that for every moment we grow,
there is a moment for rest,
so that we may grow again,
more inspired, more certain,
renewed by the light of our love.

24. Om Kapaline Namah

I will go soft. Rest easy.
I will let the darkness blanket,
but not subsume me.
Or, if I need to be subsumed,
then so I'll be.
I'll go under quietly and deeply,
knowing that in the darkness
are so many others,
hearts beating like manic drums,
weeping too, along with me.
I'll be alert to my body in space,
hold our fears and fantasies
in the soft sanctum of my belly,
take them in my arms,
and feel them pulsing under the skin,
dislodging from the caves of yesterday.
I'll rest in the darkness, and listen,
and feel the motions of change
as they course through me.
I'll imagine that each one rushing in
is a note in search of its song,
and that the song, when complete,
will bring an unbridled bliss
I have not yet known,
as the Sun begins to rise,
and seeds begin to sprout,
and we get up, and stretch,
and prepare for a new season
of earthgrown, skybound living.

25. Om Kamaraye Namah

From one season to the next,
we witness the miracle
of what comes,
and what goes.
We watch colors change,
winds and waves drift
in each of the directions.
We watch nature's creations die,
and live again,
never in the same way,
a beautiful dance,
an alchemy of transformation
without questioning why,
without resisting what fades away,
or craving new beginnings.
May I embrace change,
and find joy in the impermanence
of all things.
May I breathe through what hurts
with the fortitude of love and compassion,
knowing that it is transforming
with every breath
that breathes through time's passage
in me.

26. Om Andhakasurasudanaya Namah

May I always allow this:
the holding of my pain
as a mother holds
her newborn child,
with love,
always with love,
as an acceptance
that there will be pain
in this life
contains within it
the seeds of ease
and of healing.
Breathing in, I feel the pain.
Breathing out, I let it go.
Breathing in, I allow the pain.
Breathing out, I watch it go.

27. Om Gangadharaya Namah

I am:
the goddess
of the mountains,
the one who makes
life from life, engenders
the cycle of birth and death,
who looks upon us all with her
great gaze of transcendent wisdom
enfolding all beings in her arms of love
inviting us all to breathe her gentle fragrance
reminding us that there are no boundaries in heart.

28. Om Lalatakshaya Namah

May I learn to unsee,
in order to see.
May I close my eyes,
so that I can awaken
to a new world
with new eyes.
May I strive to undo,
in order to find
my righteous purpose
in doing.
May I stumble a little
to find my balance,
and my way upright.
May I lower myself
to the rich new earth
and lie still on the ground,
before greeting the sky.
May I fold into myself
before unleashing it all,
with my most open, loving heart,
to everything, and everyone.
May I be silent before I speak.
May I, with every gesture,
every heartbeat,
honor the incredible,
momentous chance

I've been given,
to find myself exactly here,
and exactly now,
and may I be curious,
and full of wonder,
and brave, and may we know
we are in this together.

29. Om Kalakalaya Namah

I am one with the wind, light and free.
I am one with the mountain, sure and strong.
I am one with the river, gentle and flowing.
I am one with the tree, grounded and pure.
May I always be one with the purity of the nature
around me, within me, and between us,
the greatest love story to ever be told.

30. Om Kripanid'haye Namah

I scan my body for its tensions
And, noticing them for a moment,
I breathe out, and make the bravest decision
I could make, and wonder at their departure,
knowing they were not meant to stay,
only visit long enough to remind me
that our stories are not who we are,
but steps we've taken on our path here,
beautiful steps with lessons to teach,
and that they want the same thing as us,
which is to take flight, and be free.
May I bow to the transience of all things.
May I be unafraid of the stories to come.
May I accept change with fierce bravery,
and know that I can choose my future
with every conscious breath I take.

31. Om Bhimaya Namah

May I always see beauty.
May I always hear harmonies.
May I always feel love.
May I always honor the way.
May I use my hands for giving.
May I use my heart for caring.
May I use my ears for listening.
May I use my legs for grounding.
May I use my inner eye for knowing.
May I use my voice for truth-telling.
May I live in the spirit of growing.

32. Om Parashuhastaya Namah

This is the world
I have been looking for
all of my life,
the one where goodness
lives in all the spaces
between,
shining with such vivid abandon
that it is only a matter
of time
before I can sense it,
and my body comes alive
with the delight of it,
and I realize:
it is a continuum
that defies all borders
between outside and inside,
without and within,
and one layer at a time,
I can remove the obstacles
to my true knowing,
until the goodness
flows like a tributary to the sea,
and I'll know I have found
the very core of my being.
May I forever glow
with the light of recognition
of our one true nature.

33. Om Mrigapanaye Namah

I take refuge in heart
I take refuge in wisdom
I take refuge in kindness
I take refuge in vulnerability
I take refuge in openness
I take refuge in strength
I take refuge in compassion
I take refuge in unity

May I live in the peaceful folds of my heart.
May I trust in the truths that I find there.

34. Om Jatadharaya Namah

There is no *my pain*.
There is only pain
howling a tapestry of wounds
in the moonlight,
begging us to listen.
There is no *my suffering*.
There is only suffering
standing by the roaring fire
ready to scorch and burn.
They are not mine
as long as I choose
not to surrender to their ferocity
or believe they are here
for a long and bitter communion.
No, they are not mine,
but I am with them.
We sit together by the hearth,
as I try to understand,
and the more compassion I have
for these unbidden visitors,
the less powerful they are
in the staying,
and the greater my desire
for all beings to be free.
May I understand
the shared suffering and pain
in the world,
and in learning to heal myself,
work for the healing of the world.

35. Om Kailashavasine Namah

Every day, no matter how I feel,
the Sun rises, a brilliant orb,
the Moon rises, in all her phases.
The clouds might obscure them,
but as long as we have
our life here,
they never disappear.
I see the day not as it is,
but how I am
in this one fleeting moment,
with all its contingences,
and all the ways
my heart knows how
to sing, and to break.
Some days, though,
there is a sublime moment,
and I come into my body,
and live through my breath.
These times, I catch a glimpse
of our Sun and Moon
for the brilliance that resides
within them, not as I am,
but as they are.
May I recognize wisdom and truth
in all the undying parts of my being.
May I recognize my thoughts and emotions
as clouds drifting by
before they dissolve into air and wind,
May I always return
to the heart of myself
in the heart of a world thriving.

36. Om Kawachine Namah

I heard of a place
of endless peace
where trees sway
and leaves rustle in the wind
and forest creatures rest.
For there is nothing
that needs to be done,
and no outcomes are sought
where only spirit stirs.
Will you join me there?
Let us be free together.

37. Om Kathoraya Namah

Peace
   Freedom
      Love
I'll say it again
until the words
course through my veins
like nectar,
until your pulse
knows only
these:
Peace
   Freedom
      Love
Endless peace.
Eternal freedom.
Always and only
and nothing but
love.

38. Om Tripurantakaya Namah

Can you hear it?
It's love, carried by the breeze.
It's love, swaying with the leaves.
It's love, flowing riverside by and by.
It's love, soaring with birds in the sky.
It's love, singing on the mountaintop.
It's love, dancing with each raindrop.
It's love, spreading everywhere.
It's love, laying our hearts bare.
It's love, in the heart of me.
It's love, as far as we can see.

39. Om Vrishankaya Namah

May I focus less on the objects of love,
and more on the simple, pure act of love.
May I pay less attention to love as doing,
and more to love as being.
May I live like the Sun and Moon
and the stars that are love's gift to us
and who live out their purpose
with extraordinary simplicity
in the radiant arms of love's grace.

40. Om Vrishabharudhaya Namah

May I breathe support into the bones
that hold me up.
May I breathe agility into the joints
that support my movement.
May I breathe gentleness into my back,
which carries so much.
May I breathe strength into the muscles
that grant me the magic of motion.
May I breathe discernment into my eyes
so that I may honor the shadows,
and step into the light.
May I breathe wisdom in my ears
so that I may learn how to listen.
May I breathe love into the heart
that longs to resonate
with the heart of the world.
May I breathe acceptance, compassion
and gratitude into my whole body,
this vessel for my life, soul and spirit.

41. Om Bhasmodhulitavigrahaya Namah

I breathe in—
breathing becomes laboured
snagging and catching before the end

I breathe out—
the breath becomes a cry
caught on a gasp of surprise

I sit tall—
the spine aches from holding
stories thousands of years old

I am soft—
I feel not softness but threadbare fragility
in bone and skin that threaten collapse

I am falling—
but in the falling, an acute awareness
of what I've neglected so long

I am restless—
I have within me infinite little pieces
that have been struggling to be heard

I am suffering—
I have awakened to brilliant depths
of what it means to be alive and trying
I am human—
I will ache and burn as I sit with each in turn
feeling a unity in all our pain but also our triumphs

May I learn—
that every breath in and every breath out
is a change, a chance, to live and live again.

42. Om Samaprihaya Namah

May I see
what asks to be seen.

May I love
all there is to love.

May I never stop thinking
about that which gives me pause.

May I never stop feeling
what fills and shakes my spirit.

May I never stop questioning
that which inspires confusion.

May I never stop listening
to what begs to be heard.

May I never stop doing
that which needs to get done.

May I face what I am given
fierce, kind, ready, open and sure.

43. Om Swaramayaya Namah

I am of this—

Of our fairest stars
glowing in the night
hinting at the beauty
of our mysteries

Of the orange Sun
burning its passions
like embers, falling
to our awakened skin

Of Moon above,
watchful and serene,
her rounded fullness
a perfect reflection

Of we the people
bare feet to ground,
hands to heart,
eyes gazing upward.

May I never forget
that I am this,
a wondrous communion
with all being.

44. Om Trayimurtaye Namah

Morning psalms
of gratitude
for this:
for this life,
for this breath of fire in my belly,
for the shared connections we make,
for the laughter and hope,
and for the aspiration
that we all learn to thrive,
free, at last, from our suffering
that has taught us so much.

45. Om Anishwaraya Namah

Bless the rain
and a world free of pain.
Bless the Sun's rays
and the pursuit of fulfilling days.
Bless the Moon
and a peaceful world come soon.
Bless you, and bless me,
in the work we do to be free.

46. Om Sarvajnaya Namah

Bless this day I have to start again.
Bless the day that has passed
for the lessons it has brought me.
Bless the knowledge
that everything that comes and goes,
and everything that arises,
passes away.
Bless the rebirth
that follows each small death,
for the opportunity it gives me
to find the light of new meaning.

May I always love and respect everyone
the way they deserve to be loved and respected.
May I always love and cherish myself
the way I deserve to be loved and cherished.
May I always love the world
as much as it deserves to be loved
and has always loved us without condition.

47. Om Paramatmane Namah

In a world of running
I would like to walk

In a world of noise
I would like to be silent

In a world that idolizes progress
I would like to embrace process

In a world of straight lines
I would like to find all the curves

In a world of great heights
I would like to lie close to the earth

In a world of the fleeting
I would like to dive deep and transcend

In a world of anger
I would like to find peace

In a world of conflict
I would like to find unity

In a world run by fear
I would like to burst with courage

In a world of deceptions
I would like to be a beacon of truth

In a world with too much hatred
I would like us to awaken to love together

48. Om Somasuryagnilochanaya Namah

I bless and honor
the little child inside me
who reminds me
that no matter how old I get,
no matter how hardened
by the experiences of life,
there is a part of me
that will always yearn
to shriek with laughter,
play with grasshoppers,
jump into autumn leaves
and spring puddles,
share secrets and make worlds,
sing at the top of my lungs,
ask all the wild, wise questions
and know without doubt
how very much I belong.
I love the child within
with such a deep and sudden ferocity
that my heart bursts open,
the tears begin to flow.
She has reminded me
and I can never again forget;
this love that I give so freely,
and so purely, is for me.

49. Om Havishe Namah

My heart is a flower.
It is tender, it is fragile,
it has the strength of a lion.
It came into this world
riding its own tide,
a rhythm all its own,
already imbued with knowing,
and its unceasing rhythm
bathes the world
like a crimson twilight
descending into a desert on fire,
offering solace, relief,
momentum and its own vital breath,
and it manifests a dream
as long as it is living.

Like the flower,
my heart has its time
for reaching out, and folding in,
the exquisite foundations of life.
A flower is never still;
it blossoms and grows
propelled by Earth's motions,
and finds its place
among sun and shadow,
guided by its internal rhythm
to dance to life's own,
retreating and emerging,
always coming into being.
My heart is a flower.
As long as there is life,
may it expand and contract,

may it move and feel, and guide,
and allow me to anchor
every last part of me
around its intricate, wise body,
now weaker, now stronger,
always riding the one wave of love.

50. Om Yajnamayaya Namah

Imagine if the whole world
were to exhale at once,
the long, deep breath,
the sigh, a quiver, a letting go
in profound acknowledgement
of a need for release
so strong it could cause a mountain
to give way to the sea,
a tiger to pause in his hunt,
a war to lay down its arms,
a body to glide into grace.
Imagine the shudder, a pause,
a moment of collective rest,
a small smile, finally,
finally, in surrender.
How many lifetimes will pass
in this one momentary pause,
as we arrive where we've been before,
to remember, sharing stories with our ancestors
who say, *thank you, we are freed,*
return to your place in the order of things,
please, too, be free.
And so, our hands clasp,
our feet touch sacred ground;
the heart is ready, the inhale begins.
May I breathe in,
with the world breathing in.
May I breathe out,
with the world breathing out.

51. Om Somaya Namah

I dive into my deep self
like it's an endless ocean
full of infinite wisdom,
and all the secrets I'll need.
May I honor this deep self
like the sacred ocean it is.
May I welcome life's storms
the way the earth comes alive
under the rush of pouring rain.

52. Om Panchavaktraya Namah

To the house that is not clean
and the mind that is full of clutter

To the body that aches at the joints
and the spirit in need of sunshine

To the hand afraid to reach out
and the feet afraid to take first steps,

To the fear that threatens to spill over
and the sadness that feels ancient

I send to you my deepest love
in hopes of easing your suffering.

May I always send my heartfelt love
to everything and everyone in need,

Never forgetting, too, that I exist among them
united with all that is sacred in being.

53. Om Sadashivaya Namah

Mystery
is the most beautiful word.
It is right there,
between every layer
of skin,
the casting of all shadows.
It is around the corner
of your known destination,
just in front of,
and behind the fixed gaze.
It is everything you thought
you knew
and put comfortably
behind you,
and all the things
never considered,
but feared, anticipated,
wondered at and contemplated,
for hours on end,
with a soft and curious heart.
May the known
take you on a journey
to the not yet known.
May what is visible
remind you
of all you cannot yet see.

54. Om Vishveshwaraya Namah

May I let go of the need
to put everything into words
and then into action.
May I surrender to the sublime nature
of the here and now,
where, beyond words and actions,
before sight and sound,
there is pure presence of being,
mingling with our true
and forever selves.

55. Om Virabhadraya Namah

The sounds of the cosmos in each breath,
the limitlessness of beauty in each expansion,
the invitation of possibility in every inhalation,
the unfolding of worlds in every exhalation.
May I always invite a universe of possibility.
May I always open to the universe freely.

56. Om Gananathaya Namah

I breathe as Sun's rays
emerge from parting clouds,
and I breathe with the raindrops
falling silently to the ground.
I breathe to the rhythm
of belly laughter under the stars
and to the tears and silent prayers
only the Moon can know.
I breathe this all in.
I breathe it all out.
I startle at life's ability
to arrest me with her wonders
from beginning to end,
and back to the very beginning again.

57. Om Prajapataye Namah

In this moment, I am free.
In this moment,
yesterday has taken flight,
and there is no hint of tomorrow.
There is nothing left to regret,
no hint of remaining fear.
There is only now,
pure and fleeting.
My body is alive;
it thrums with the pulse
of the living,
in harmony with
life's unceasing motion.
May I breathe this moment in,
and breathe this moment out,
unleashing it to the wind,
watching it disappear.
May I feel the lightness
that enters my body,
where once burdens grew,
and may the lightness spread to all,
in the one name of love.

58. Om Hiranyaretase Namah

Here are my hands, soft and warm,
here is the earth, accepting them.
Here are my arms, relaxed and loose,
here is the earth, accepting them.
Here is my head, spacious and full,
here is the earth, accepting it.
Here is my back, raw and exposed,
here is the earth, accepting it.
Here is my heart, growing and learning,
here is the earth, accepting it.
Here are my legs, strong and rooted,
here is the earth, accepting them.
Here are my feet, bare and curious,
here is the earth, accepting them.
Here is my body, slowly relaxing,
here is the earth, accepting it.
Here is my body, now tense, now still,
here is the earth, accepting it.
Here is my body, surrendering in full,
here is the earth, always accepting.

59. Om Durdʹharshaya Namah

May the world's sounds reach me
in their sweet and full roundedness.
May the world's visions reach me
in their rich and vibrant luminosity.
May I always resonate with the rhythms
of the most intimate, numinous dance.

60. Om Girishaya Namah

Run wild and free, then take rest.
Roar on the mountain peaks, and then rest.
Fling yourself into the ocean's wild waves, and rest.
While resting, hold velvety flowers in your hands.
Laugh until your belly is empty, and rest again.
Cry the hurt out and the ruins away,
until it's time to rest.
May I always find time to play and express,
and honor my need to pause
so that I may bring my very best self
to everything I am blessed to do,
and to all I am blessed to be.

61. Om Girishaya Namah II

If I can't remove your pain,
let me hold it, gently, with you,

If I can't walk your path,
let me walk alongside you,

If I can't inhabit your body,
let me cast my love on it,

If I can't efface your self-judgment,
let me be your gentle touch,

If I can't forage for your treasures,
let me share my own with you,

If I can't get you out of the dark,
let me be your reservoir of light,

And if I find myself in your shoes,
if I need the same kindness as you,

Let me remember to find you,
let me allow you in, too.

62. Om Anaghaya Namah

In a torrent of rain,
the grace of a single raindrop.
In winter's greatest snow,
the exquisite beauty of a single snowflake.
May I always seek grace.
May I remember where beauty lies.
May I remember that we can find
beauty's terrain everywhere,
and that it is for everyone
to receive, and to make.

63. Om Bujanabhushanaya Namah

The house I will build for you
will not always be the most perfect
or well-kept house

It will not always be standing
as firmly as you need it to,
upon its foundation of good intentions

It will at times shake and shiver
as the winds howl into gales
that have all the markers of rage

It might sigh and tremble and
start to collapse in certain parts
as though doubt itself built its joints

And the waters running beneath
will seep into its skin and bones
and threaten to drown the house

That we have constructed with all
the love we know how to put
into things with our well-meaning hands

Things that we want so badly
to hold in firm, warm embrace
and never let go of, and never leave
But this house I will build for you
will always persevere, because the
blood of generations runs through

Its sometimes strong and sometimes
wavering frame, and it beats and it
thrums until we recognize the dance

And the view from all sides will
always be untarnished, and the horizons
of love will always keep it standing.

64. Om Bhargaya Namah

May each moment be infused
with transcendence,
and may I recognize
that the sublime is always within me.
May I live with love
every moment of every day,
with those I love and who love me,
with the air I breathe,
with the life I live.
May I also honor a love
that is unconditional,
our birthright and legacy,
and our true path to freedom.

65. Om Giridhanvane Namah

As I rest my body, mind and soul,
a peace envelops me, wide and deep.
Within this silence, I watch the rise
of ancient emotions, thoughts and feelings,
like the ruins of gloried temples,
and I hold them with love and acceptance.
May I always embrace every single part
of who I was, who I am, and who I will be.

66. Om Giripriyaya Namah

There are times I long for things
beyond the horizon,
when my gaze knows no bounds,
when my dreams take me
anywhere but here.
Ah, but I am here.
May I answer to my dreams
from exactly where I am,
in this space, in this home,
in this body, mind and spirit,
in the present moment,
happy and in perfect communion
with this one true moment in time.

67. Om Krittivasase Namah

If I feel behind today,
I forgive myself.
If I forget to be present,
I forgive myself.
If I let anger and fear overcome me,
I forgive myself.
If I compare myself with others,
I forgive myself.
If I am full of doubts that consume me,
I forgive myself.
May I always be full of forgiveness,
for myself and for others.
May I remember that how I feel today
is not how it will be tomorrow,
and that every day
is ripe with new creation.

68. Om Purarayaye Namah

The clouds reveal my dreams,
when I am looking.
The trees whisper their secrets,
when I am listening.
The mountains teach me of strength,
when I allow them into my view.
The ocean soothes and heals me,
when I enter her silky embrace.
May I always place my self
in the gentle arms
of the world's power and serenity,
and come awake through
each of my senses
that have so much to teach me
about the world around me,
and my place in it,
as I seek full immersion
in the very heart of existence.

69. Om Bhagawate Namah

In my pain,
there is a beautiful opening.
My body, mind and spirit
have a lesson for me,
and I am here to learn.
I am here not just to understand,
but to observe and to feel,
to allow the pain to merge
into my experience of living,
and as it has come, it will go.
May I not turn away in aversion
to that which has so much to teach me
before it disappears,
in the way of all things.
May I journey through the pain with courage,
and revel in the peace that follows.

70. Om Pramathadhipaya Namah

May I awaken
in this very moment
to the soft earth under my feet,
humming with life
where my body touches ground,
even as I seek
the highest skies.
May I understand
deep within me
that when I can't breathe,
and the ground feels far away,
I will still not fall.
I will still, always,
have this place to go,
that I am protected,
embraced, accepted,
and loved
by the Earth
from where I come.

71. Om Mrityunjayaya Namah

The forest is dark and inviting.
I enter through a winding trail,
and follow the scent of the trees.
My bare feet meet the deep rich earth
as I walk through the forest deep.
And then I stop, and close my eyes,
and remember that we call home from here.
The earth, the trees, the sky, the river rushing by,
are everything I have been striving for.
I close my eyes
and let home speak through my heart.
May I always listen from the purest place
inside of me
and remember where I am from
and where my true home is:
where I will always be confident
and utterly unafraid to be me.

72. Om Sukshmatanave Namah

For my mother,
for my father,
for the miracle
of my birth,
in this place
and this time,
knowing how unlikely
it is
that I am here
at all,
how many things
had to happen,
and work together
all at once
for me to arrive,
that this is the miracle
of being,
and for this,
I bow
in deep gratitude.

73. Om Jagadvyapine Namah

May I always see with new eyes,
like a baby enthralled with the world.
May I always see with my whole heart
that the light in me reflects the light
of every being and of all that is,
just as the river of light reflects my glow
back to me when I forget to see.

Take me on a path that has no name,
teach me to sing from my belly
and to dance fiercely and recklessly.
Show me the space between two stars
and help me forget that I am yearning,
and let us dip into the deepest waters,
and know beyond knowing that we live.

74. Om Jagadguruve Namaḥ

I look to the moments behind me,
and smile in thanks for the gifts
they have given me
as my heritage and my legacy.
I look forward to the moments ahead
in gleeful anticipation for what they might be,
and where they will take me.
Then I turn right back to the present moment,
in full awareness
that this is where life can be lived,
appreciated, enjoyed and fulfilled.
May I live each moment
with a powerful presence of being,
with no thought of yesterday,
or tomorrow, or any moment
that takes me away from where I am,
in the beautiful space of my body
that works with elegance,
precision and sophistication to make
the magic of being so effortless,
and peaceful communion with all beings
the greatest offering of our humanity.

75. Om Vyomakeshaya Namah

I am not the person
I was yesterday.
I am not the person
I will be tomorrow.
I awaken today
to a new Sun, in a new sky,
knowing I have died
a thousand deaths
to get here,
and I will die a thousand more,
as I move toward
my beautiful evolution.

Teach me, Moon,
to accept the truths
as they come.
Guide me to know
not to fear the shadows.
Show me
how to see softly,
how to glow brightly
in the dark.
Thank you, Moon,
for your giving.
For the light of night,
for your reflections.

76. Om Mahasenajanakaya Namah

There are more pathways
into the depths of the forest
than we can see or imagine
when we first venture in.
My body knows;
I shiver with delight and excitement
as the paths diverge.
May I go deeply and boldly
into this forest of life,
and be unafraid of what
I will find there.
May I discover
the perfect pathway
for my growth and discovery
as I learn to touch within me
each of the elements:
earth, water, fire, air and ether.
May love light them all.

77. Om Charuvikramaya Namah

What is the essence
of something,
if not the part of it
always ready
to spread its wings and soar,
the part that is filled with hope
for a better tomorrow,
and a smile for today?
May I live in humble gratitude
not only for that which
is always changing,
but for what is eternal
and unchanging
in us all.
Which is what loves.
Which is always love.

78. Om Rudraya Namah

In the new dawn,
dewdrops blanket the world,
and the clouds drift and float
to make way for blue skies.
The Sun peeks through
the mountaintops,
and the path forward alights.
I brush my dreams away,
breathe deep, and stretch,
until I am more
than I usually allow
myself to be.
This is this the perfection
of a moment
without history or expectation.
This is the portal
through which everything else is born.
May I take this day into my arms.
May I ask nothing of this day,
which unfolds with great wisdom.
May I be available to this day
with playful exploration,
daring adventures,
ginger curiosity,
and ineffable joy.

79. Om Bhutapataye Namah

On soft ground,
Mama Earth speaks for
each of us.
I am soft, too, she says,
in my strength that bears no rigidity.
Life rises through me
because I know without knowing
where I stand,
what I stand upon,
when it is time to rest.
Life lives within me
as I aim, not higher
than can sustain me,
but to be a perfect reflection
of who I am here, and now.
And for the Sun, the trees, water,
the air that brushes across my surfaces
and echoes the expanse
of vast spaces inside,
my gratitude,
for making ground and heavens
of this present moment,
for both giving and surrendering
to the wonder of the whole universe
within each life in open stillness.

80. Om Sthanave Namah

I fold my heart in,
protecting what is tender
and hurt and holy.
There is a softness
dear and beloved;
there is a time for
this fragile quietude.
Then I reach back
and thrust my heart
out to the day that greets me,
ready for the shining light
to stream in,
ready to be a pure
vessel of love.
May I always be
a kind, compassionate witness
to the ebb and flow,
to the rhythms of love
as they arise,
and they always will.
Love always does.

81. Om Ahirbudʿhnyaya Namah

Behind the one, the all.
I stand here, now,
taking this one breath,
and the next.
I find, in the spaces
between breathing in
and breathing out,
that there is a pause,
a briefest moment
of contemplation and reckoning,
as a part of me decides,
yes, I am going to continue.
I am going to go on.
I am going to wander,
journey, meander, and find.
I will traverse the path of life,
beginning with this one
momentous breath
that seems to fill the world,
and know that I am doing so
on the back of those
who came before me,
those most loving, intimate,
profound parts of my birthright,
so that they are the earth
from which I spring,
the waters from which I emerge,
bold and unafraid,
the song I come to remember
that I have always known.

We are here, they tell me,
not to hold you back,
but to whisper to you,
in every breath,
in freeing yourself,
you free us too.
You are the love of our times.
Go embrace this love
with every single one of your gifts,
in the name of the one great love,
in all of our names,
in the one great sound.
What a wonder,
to have so much in a breath.

82. Om Digambaraya Namah

On days when the world feels like
a mountain crumbling under the weight
of the blackest, stormiest skies,
when the stories we tell ourselves
also fall, no longer working for us
the way we thought they would,
there is one thing we can do,
and it's always been our ally:
we can turn to the breath.
We can breathe in love,
and breathe out what aches.
Again and again,
we can breathe love in,
until something special happens,
and we breathe love out.
Deep, full inhalation,
Soft, long exhalation.
May I breathe through
all that life brings,
and not wish for things
to be other than they are,
and may I awaken to what is fresh
and beautiful as new life begins.

83. Om Ashtamurtaye Namah

My body,
a brilliant vessel
of possibility,
sacred home,
valley and carrier
for the divine.
The wondrous crevices,
the curves, the sinews.
The skin, its lines,
each a smile
from the universe, saying,
your experiences matter.
Breathe in light,
breathe out darkness.
Breathe in color,
breathe out what is dull and grey.
May I infuse my body with brightness
and honor the divine
within me.

84. Om Anekatmane Namah

The breath that knows no breath
The step that knows not it treads
The shadow unaware of the dark
The growth that sees not its rise

The Sun that does not light itself
The Moon free of her revolutions
The Earth that has not a home
The sky that fears not its falling

Until I can take you to this place
where, in this way, we are free
I stand with you, hold your hand
and honor who you are, as I am.

85. Om Satvikaya Namah

The Moon round and full,
bears her ancient secrets,
and moves the oceans
with her wisdom and her own,
secret knowing of time.

May I know the unbridled joy
of bathing under the moonlight,
closing my eyes and smiling,
and sharing in her wisdom,
which is available to us all
and can never be destroyed.

86. Shuddhavigrahaya Namah

On a path that is
true and sincere,
everything becomes
a temple
with its hallowed spaces
for knowing,
and a garden
that blooms wild and free
and has never
run out of patience,
and a tree that will never
stoop in defeat.
A time will come
when we understand
these qualities
as our own
and we will humble ourselves
at what lies before us
and to what lies within.
May I bow in servitude
and in preparation
for this most holy of moments.

87. Om Shashvataya Namah

I delight in absurdities;
there is no tomorrow.
I seek out the diamond rain;
it will not be here again.
I mix the sacred and frivolous,
puncture each moment
of darkness's depths
with wells of profound joy,
even if the inner bell rings
to say it's all too much,
or never, ever enough,
that there are other things
that need to be done.
I know deep within me
that there is nothing
that needs doing,
that we craft need like an art
every time we wake up
in yesterday's cocoon,
enveloped in expectations
from our selves now past.
No, instead, I carry the wisdom,
drop the leaden fear,
pierce through every last shadow,
all the dusty remains,
flip the switch, become silly,
sift for what is golden,
what makes every heart sing,
and merge my life to yours.
The song of my life
comes from the fire sun,
and it was written just for me.

88. Om Khandaparashave Namah

Imagine if life were just a little longer,
so that we could paint more of our experiences
onto the unfolding landscape perpetually receding
deeper and deeper into the growing distance

before we can grab it, never to let go.

Imagine if life were just a little shorter,
so that we could lay on fertile ground
those worries we have about all that awaits us,
the interminable stretch of years to be filled

that, if we are honest, we still fear losing.

Imagine if just like that, the perspective shifted,
and life were exactly what it was, and we as we are,
and notions of time faded into the beautiful ether
as we find ourselves reaching no further than here

in the happiness of living embodied and true.

✾

May all that I imagine serve my greatest good.
May I live in gratitude for everything my path shows me.

89. Om Ajaya Namah

Come
sit with me.
I want to say,
it's been such a long time.

Maybe this place is unfamiliar to you,
I know—I am also, still, not so sure of it,
or even how I came to be here.

I'm not sure which of my histories
had to emerge, defiant and victorious,
from the rest, for today to take
the shape it has, or why,

Or how to contend with
my other stories, so stubborn and sure,
each cropping up, in turn,
to ask something of me.

Maybe it's like that for you, too,
where you are?
I would like to meet you there
and hear your stories.

I would like for the act
of our communion, though,
to be our beginning,
to form the core of our existence,
both yours and mine,
And for the stories
to enlighten us without taking over.

Let us sit together,
and not scramble for meaning,
or dismiss the struggle either.

Let us take all of it,
hold it in the space between us,
and breathe and love and be,
you, and me,

And start
from the only place we can,
here, and now,
all we have ever needed.

90. Om Pashavimochakaya Namah

Sometimes the breadth
of our wounds
is all I can see,
and I gasp to see it.
Sometimes, a strip of sunlight
slips in through the window
and cascades into the room
and suddenly, the wounds
begin to ease,
so that I may confront them
with a soft and brilliant peace.
May I awaken every day
to the knowledge that
things never stay the same,
and welcome the beauty
of this everlasting truth.

91. Om Mridaya Namah

I awaken to joy,
I awaken to sorrow,
I awaken to wonderment,
and I awaken to bewilderment.
I awaken to everything in its right place,
and I awaken to confusion and chaos.
The important thing is that I awaken,
everyday, to a beautiful new world.
May I always awaken.
May I always remember the possibility
of awakening new, to each and every
part of our glorious now.

92. Om Pashupataye Namah

Everywhere we go,
under every rock,
between each blade of grass,
streaming through the juices
of trees and moss,
there are the beating hearts
that protect us.
It's in the wind, too,
how it whispers
through each of us,
and never discriminates.
It's in every pathway
that welcomes
every being
to find its way here.
May we find that which
loves us,
and that which is love,
in all places, and all beings.

93. Om Devaya Namah

A love without boundaries,
one that sees directly from heart,
one love that we share,
as all of us here share
this place that houses us,
this space, this time.
It is a love that expands
as we breathe into it,
as we hold hands
and attend to each movement,
slowly, assuredly, in peace.
May I embrace universal love,
and share all my love
with the world.

94. Om Mahadevaya Namah

I give deep thanks to this body of mine,
the blood that streams with wild abandon
along pathways generating the cycles of life,
the bones, supple and strong, that hold me up,
the feet that allow me to touch ground and travel far,
the hands that allow me to create, and bring others close,
the organs that are working day and night to sustain me,
the skin that holds me together and protects me,
sheltering me as I explore and touch this beautiful land,
the eyes and ears, nose and mouth
that bring a vast array of sensations to my being
and help me celebrate the joy of being alive.
May I always be grateful for this body of mine,
this sacred house that I live in,
this conduit between myself and the unbound world.

95. Om Avyayaya Namah

Today, I will surrender to my fear
of all that is uncertain.
Today, I will surrender to my feelings
of discomfort and unease.
Today, I will breathe into what ails me
and trust in my body's ability to heal.
Today, I surrender,
grateful for the harmony between myself
and the Sun, Moon, water and Earth.
May I always find it in my heart
to yield in gratitude for everything
I have been given,
and that I still have to give.

96. Om Haraye Namah

How lucky I am
to have a ground
so firm and dependable
under my feet

Such vibrant, old
and wise beings
in my midst every
way I look

Distant lands
I can hardly
dream of, ready for
my evolution

And always the sky,
keeper of my
secrets and dreams
until, finally, I arrive.

May the road
to happiness and bliss
be full of
sublime adventure.

97. Om Bhaganetrabhide Namah

In gratitude, I stretch my limbs
feeling the space between bones
as they sigh and let go.
With love, I breathe deeper
into those expanding spaces,
allowing them the space to be.
I close my eyes and listen
for the story my changing body
would like to tell me,
and hear every thought and feeling
with a warm and kind receiving.
May I always remain open
to everyone and every story
with love instead of judgment.

98. Om Avyaktaya Namah

Soft around the edges I go,
it is not too cold or too warm,
the colors are gentle and inviting,
and there is a lulling breeze.
In the center, our life-giving Sun
beams on a tall tree on a rounded hill.
The tree has more power
than I've ever imagined or known,
but it is also quiet, and still,
and speaks fluidly of peace
more than anything I've seen,
or words ever could.
Life's source streams through it
from root to rustling leaf;
the tree rests in pure being,
inviting me to try the same.

Many nights I gaze up at the Moon,
looking for a sign that I am ready
to stop my journey around the edges,
and one night, when the Moon is full,
I know the time has come,
and something has changed inside of me.
I look toward the tree and smile.
The ground is solid under my feet
and I know that I am safe.
I give thanks for where I've been
as I take my first steps toward the tree,
hesitant at first, and then, more free.

The Moon's glow lights my path
as I climb, a new and true warrior of light,
connecting to the source of all life.
May I rest in strength and confidence
with each step I take toward source.
May I be guided on my way there.

99. Om Dakshadhwaraharaya Namah

I see a wall in the distance.
I approach tenderly,
with small, careful steps.
Up close I see gems
the colors of antiquity
and the greatest stories
ever told by all the great sages,
smiles like ivory and pearl.
Contemplating the wall
before me, I see alchemy,
concrete turned to art,
or the skin of a mermaid,
awash in the depths
of our collective awakening,
and I am transported.
May I always learn as I stumble,
and as I keep
my eye and heart
on the glories unseen.

100. Om Haraya Namah

The light that is in us all
grows with every breath
we inhale, with all the love
we pour into the world.
They are not miracles that we seek,
for miracles hint of the impossible,
but love is the world of infinite potential,
and it is the grasp of us all.
As we stretch and open
to the space of love,
as we make room in our hearts
for endless joy to stream in,
we shine a light on everything
we ever dreamed we needed,
and on the sacred holiness
that is always surrounding us.
May I open the sacred door to love
and realize the miracles
that always dwell as without, within.

101. Om Pushadantabhide Namah

I stand on the green grass below,
feet rooted in the soft, lush earth.
I feel a surge of energy
coursing through me,
from the tips of my toes
up my body to the crown of my head,
and know that I am grounded,
and know that I am here, safe,
between Earth below and skies above.
I allow spirit to flow through me.
I listen to the rhythms of my body,
breathing love into places of need,
giving thanks where it is light and free.
When I feel the spirit rise,
I let it rise. And it always does,
and it always will.
May I always, with grace,
allow my spirit to rise.

102. Om Avyagraya Namah

Only love
can be all things
and the space between them,
as though it spills over
from every hopeful part of us,
joyful, to spread the message
that we've had it all wrong,
and there is only good,
and it is all perfect,
and the message is received
so that the space around things,
before long,
remembers only love,
and makes the love of things
that much more luminous,
and the Sun, of course,
is filled with love,
carried over
from the Moon's smiling departure
as we dream our love-filled dreams,
and so, we awaken,
and may we always awaken
to a sea of the love
inside of us,
in a world transformed by love.

103. Om Sahasrakshaya Namah

Find your heart in the forest,
for it whispers there between trees
reaching up to the eternal sky.
There it sings among the crackling,
brown leaves carpeting the ground
with the pine needles, moss and stone.
The heart of us all weaves through
the space between leaves,
right there in a bird's song.
We enter into the darkness of the forest
and come to places streaming with light,
and if we listen carefully enough,
there it is: the purity of being,
the source of what and who we are.
May I hear my heart beating
in the silence all around me,
and I know that I am here,
and know that I am all that is.

104. Om Sahasrapade Namah

I focus on the spaces between:
between my eyes, between my hands,
between body, thought and feeling.
Between the ground and gloried sky
is where source moves through us,
the realm of our creation and growth.
As I rest my attention on the in-between,
I discover the most remarkable thing:
that *here* and *there* dissolves,
that there is no ground and no sky,
no separation between body and mind.
Instead, an explosion of endless space,
its origin in one precious, gemlike place,
the heart of all things.
It is always the heart, in all things.
May I learn to live with heart,
so that my vision can keep growing
until differences dissolve and I rest in unity.

105. Om Apavargapradaya Namah

There is a universe blooming inside me,
powerful, expansive and divine-originating,
and I follow her call, as she follows mine,
for the only language is the song of one.
And so we go to where the trails unfold,
knowing that we will be delicately guided
to the oceans, fields, skies and mountains
that breathe life into this venerable world,
where we will confront our deepest selves,
mirrored in nature's everlasting splendor,
and know that our nature, too, is purity,
and that our explorations will take us far.
May I always intuit the universe within me,
and be unafraid to seek nature's wisdom.

106. Om Anantaya Namah

Where the wild flower lives,
the joy of perfect stillness.

Where the grass becomes
our verdant and safe harbor

and amid such greatness,
we can bow with humility

And allow our gentle undoing.
And so, happily, we fall.

May I allow myself to trust
what's safe to hold me.

May I fall with grace,
knowing I will rise again.

107. Om Tarakaya Namah

A message from one heart
to another:
walk in peace,
and know that peace
is your authentic homeland.
Walk in trust,
knowing you won't be let down.
Walk among your highest aspirations,
knowing your dreams are supported.
Walk with faith,
and be assured you are safe.
Walk with love,
knowing you are always
with love and in love's kind arms.
From all your yesterdays
to all your tomorrows.
may we delve deeper and deeper
into the light of our own being
and take tender steps
with respect for all life, and in harmony
with all of life's beautiful beings.

108. Om Parameshwaraya Namah

Celebrate!
There are your feet treading the forest floor,
you have announced your arrival to the world.
You have, guided by the Moon, reached the ocean,
you have bathed in the waves of creation and sensuous relationship.
You have been guided by the Sun to find the horizon,
you have etched the world with your strong, beautiful will.
There are your hands clasped at your heart,
you have seen, felt and experienced the vastness of your love.
There is the startling voice that is all your own,
you have found the keys to the song of the universe.
You have now arrived at the eye turned inward,
your wisdom and intuition are lit from within.
And here you are, seated at cosmic consciousness.
you have arrived, glorious, powerful, happy and free.

Now bring your hand to heart, and say:

May I celebrate each and every divine-given day,
and find love in my journey every step of the way.

EPILOGUE

Three Meditations

1. Did You Know?

Did you know that if you took all the blood vessels in your beautiful body, and joined them end-to-end, you could create a string that wraps around the world, twice? Do you feel the power of that? That you have the whole world, twice, contained in the water, the blood and the plasma of your being, and that it is thumping, pounding, seeking resonance, too? Can you feel how very much a heart full of love would heal, how it would soak into our land surfaces and flow into rivers and oceans, and absorb, and circulate, and how both would be cleansed, and how we would all heal, together? You have worlds full of love nestled in the holy space of your body, and how can you not know how very powerful you are?

2. Lamentations

The letter I never sent you.
The lonely cry in the night.

The star flickering to fade.
The dog crawling away to die.

The love I couldn't give you.
Your fear of things in the dark.

The shadows eating the day.
The storm we didn't predict.

The answers I never found.
The questions I never asked.

The fade of the photo's colors.
The rewriting of storied joy.

Sense fracturing at the edges.
The inability to know what's true.

A baby's unanswered wail.
A mother's heart ripped open.

The time we thought we had.
Laying remembrance to dust.

These are twilight's laments
How often their power sounds.

Here is the forest, inviting us.
To go deep, to emerge again.

3. I Choose Love

When it turns to dark
and my heart says hide,
I can still love.
When I can't inspire
or feel the muse around me,
still, I can love.

When the air has gone dry,
when my throat is muffled,
when I can no longer sing,
I can still choose love.

When the words fail me,
when everything is wrecked,
when love has forsaken me
and my memories fade
so that I'm forsaking myself,
there is still a space for love.

When my soul fragments,
when my joints thicken in fury,
when my eyes gloss over
and I can hear the ocean wailing,
when the world is torn to bits,
I can still love, and love again.

When the magic fades away,
when I've lost my perspective,
when my protection is gone
and my nerves are shot,
when the tears won't stop,
when I never want them to,
I can always choose love.

When the sky hangs heaviest,
when fear is the loudest sound,
when I collapse into a pile
and passions run mad,
when colours bleed and spill,
I can choose the path of love.

When the platform is gone,
when I don't understand
anything at all about love,
I will still, as best as I can,
choose love.

BONUS

Three little stories for children
(and the children inside us all)

I Really Like You

I have to tell you something.

I like you.

I don't just like you.

I really like you.

There are so many great things that make you you.

I like all the things I like about you.

I even like all the things I don't get at first.

Because they make you different from me.

And it's good to be different.

If everything was the same all the time,

it would be so boring.

I like that you're different from me,

because I can learn things from you

that I don't already know,

like why you like what you do,

and then I can like them too.

And then I can like more things,

and there will be more things to like.

I like what makes you unique and special.

You're like a magic fun box full of secret treasures,

and maybe I can be like that for you too.

I would like to get to know you better,

because I already like you.

But then I can like you even more,

and the world will be filled with so much liking.

So let me say it again:

I really like you,

and I am so happy to know you,

because you're special

and because you are you.

I Wish You the Best

Can I tell you something
from the bottom of my heart?
It's not a secret,
but maybe you can come extra close,
so I can hug you when I tell you.
What I want to say is:
I wish you the best.
I always want the best for you.
The very best.
All the best things.
The biggest piece of cake at the birthday party.
The most amazing friends to always cheer you up.
The most fun day at the park.
The very best presents.
The best rides at the amusement park.
But not only those kinds of things.
Bigger things, even if you can't see them.
I wish for your happiness.
I want you to be happy all the time.
I want you not to hurt or feel sad.
I want the whole entire world
to be full of magical things
for you to have fun and play with.
I want you to find help
whenever you need it

and to always be safe and cozy.
Even though we don't always agree about things.
Even though to be honest,
I also want the best things for me.
But I also really want the best things for you.
Because even though we're different,
we are also the same.
We are both human beings,
and we want to be happy
and we want to not be sad.
In this way we are the same.
We both have wishes and dreams.
We have the same heart,
that sometimes races fast
and sometimes goes nice and slow,
and it loves people
like I love you
and you love me.
Because of all these things,
I wish you the best.
I wish you all the very best of everything
for now and always and forever.

I Have a Secret to Tell You

I have a secret.
But now I want to share it with you.
It's a pretty big secret.
Actually, I think it's the biggest secret ever.
But you are so nice and you are my friend,
so I want to tell it to you,
because I know you will listen to me
and give me a great big hug
if I need it.
(I will need it).
My secret is this:
I'm scared.
I'm scared of so many things!
I'm scared of the dark.
I'm scared of the monsters hiding in the dark.
I'm afraid of how big the great wide world is.
I'm afraid I'm going to get lost in the huge world,
and no one will be able to find me.
I'm scared that I won't grow big and tall and strong.
I'm afraid that I am not good enough.
I'm afraid that the people who love me
will stop loving me,
and that I'll be left all alone.
I'm afraid of big things and small things.
I'm afraid of things that are close by
and things that are far away.
I'm scared of things that are real
and I'm scared of things
that people say are not real.
Sometimes I'm even afraid of my own shadow!
Whew! That was my secret.
I was so afraid to tell you all these things.

But now that I told you,
I feel so much better.
My fears felt like big dark bubbles
filling up all my insides,
until I could hardly breathe.
But now that I said them out loud to you,
I can feel them getting smaller inside of me,
like all they needed was for me to say them,
for them to lose their huge enormous power.
Now they are words that float into the air,
and float all the way up to the sky,
where they can disappear.
What's that?
You are afraid of these things too?
I'm not the only one?
I'm so relieved!
I don't want to you be sad and afraid,
but if we feel the same way,
maybe we can be scared together,
and we can be a little less scared.
I would like that very much.
Let's take paper and crayons,
and draw our fears,
and then we can see
that they are not so scary after all,
once we can look at them
and talk about them.
And we can put the drawing away,
and then we can go play,
and find all the good and fun things in the world,
that are not scary at all
because there are so many more of those
than scary things.
Thank you for listening to me,
I feel so much better now!

Appendix: The 108 Names of Hindu Deity Shiva

1	Om Shivaya Namah	Always Pure
2	Om Maheshwaraya Namah	Lord Of Gods
3	Om Shambhave Namah	One Who Bestows Prosperity
4	Om Pinakine Namah	One Who Has A Bow In His Hand
5	Om Shashishekharaya Namah	The God Who Wears The Crescent Moon In His Hair
6	Om Vamadevaya Namah	The God Who Is Pleasing And Auspicious In Every Way
7	Om Virupakshaya Namah	Lord Shiva With Oblique Eyes
8	Om Kapardine Namah	The Lord With Thickly Matted Hair
9	Om Nilalohitaya Namah	The One With Red And Blue Colour
10	Om Shankaraya Namah	One Who Gives Happiness And Prosperity
11	Om Shulapanaye Namah	The One Who Carries A Trident

12	Om Khatvangine Namah	The God Who Carries A Knurled Club (Khatvanga)
13	Om Vishnuvallabhaya Namah	The One Who Is Dear To Lord Vishnu
14	Om Shipivishtaya Namah	The Lord Whose Form Emits Great Rays Of Light
15	Om Ambikanathaya Namah	Consort Of Ambika (Parvati)
16	Om Shrikanthaya Namah	Of Glorious Neck
17	Om Bhaktavatsalaya Namah	The One Who Is Favourably Inclined Towards His Devotees
18	Om Bhavaya Namah	The God Who Is Existence Itself
19	Om Sharvaya Namah	Remover Of All Troubles
20	Om Trilokeshaya Namah	The Lord Of All The Three Worlds
21	Om Shitikanthaya Namah	The Lord Who Has White Neck
22	Om ShivaPriyaya Namah	Beloved Of Parvati
23	Om Ugraya Namah	The One Who Has Extremely Fierce Nature
24	Om Kapaline Namah	One Who Wears A Necklace Of Skulls
25	Om Kamaraye Namah	Enemy Of Kamadeva
26	Om Andhakasurasudanaya Namah	The Lord Who Killed The Asura Andhaka

27	Om Gangadharaya Namah	The God Who Holds The Ganges River In His Hair
28	Om Lalatakshaya Namah	One Who Has An Eye In The Forehead
29	Om Kalakalaya Namah	He Is The Death Of Death
30	Om Kripanidhaye Namah	The God Who Is The Treasure Of Compassion
31	Om Bhimaya Namah	The One Who Has Fearful Form
32	Om Parashuhastaya Namah	The God Who Holds Axe In Hands
33	Om Mrigapanaye Namah	The God Who Possess Deer In Hands
34	Om Jatadharaya Namah	The God Who Keeps Tress (Jata)
35	Om Kailashavasine Namah	Native Of Kailasha
36	Om Kawachine Namah	The God Who Possess Armour
37	Om Kathoraya Namah	The God Who Has A Strong Body
38	Om Tripurantakaya Namah	The God Who Killed Tripurasura
39	Om Vrishankaya Namah	The God Who Has A Flag With A Symbol Of Bull
40	Om Vrishabharudhaya Namah	The One Who Rides Bull

41	Om Bhasmodhulitavigrahaya Namah	The One Who Applies Ashes All Over The Body
42	Om Samapriyaya Namah	The One Who Loves With Equality
43	Om Swaramayaya Namah	The God Who Lives In All Seven Notes
44	Om Trayimurtaye Namah	The One Who Possess Veda Form
45	Om Anishwaraya Namah	The One Who Does Not Have Any Lord
46	Om Sarvajnaya Namah	The One Who Knows Everything
47	Om Paramatmane Namah	Everyone's Own Soul
48	Om Somasuryagnilochanaya Namah	The One Who Has Eyes In The Form Of Sun, Moon And Fire
49	Om Havishe Namah	He Who Is Wealthy In The Form Of Ahuti
50	Om Yajnamayaya Namah	The Architect Of All Sacrificial Rites
51	Om Somaya Namah	The One Who Includes The Form Of Uma
52	Om Panchavaktraya Namah	God Of The Five Activities
53	Om Sadashivaya Namah	The One Who Is Eternally Auspicious
54	Om Vishveshwaraya Namah	Lord Of The Universe

55	Om Virabhadraya Namah	Who Is Violent, Yet Peaceful
56	Om Gananathaya Namah	God Of The Ganas
57	Om Prajapataye Namah	The One Who Is The Creator Of Dynasty
58	Om Hiranyaretase Namah	The One Who Emanates Golden Souls
59	Om Durdharshaya Namah	The One Who Is Unconquerable
60	Om Girishaya Namah	Lord Of Mountains
61	Om Girishaya Namah	The God Who Sleeps On Kailash Mountain
62	Om Anaghaya Namah	He Who Is Pure
63	Om Bujangabhushanaya Namah	Lord Adorned With Golden Snakes
64	Om Bhargaya Namah	Lord Who Ends All Sins
65	Om Giridhanvane Namah	God Whose Weapon Is A Mountain
66	Om Giripriyaya Namah	Lord Who Is Fond Of Mountains
67	Om Krittivasase Namah	God Who Wears Clothes Of Elephant Skin
68	Om Purarataye Namah	Destroyer OF Town Or "Pur" Named Enemy

69	Om Bhagawate Namah	God Of Prosperity
70	Om Pramathadhipaya Namah	God Who Is Served By Goblins
71	Om Mrityunjayaya Namah	Victor Of Death
72	Om Sukshmatanave Namah	God Who Has A Subtle Body
73	Om Jagadvyapine Namah	God Who Lives In The World
74	Om Jagadguruve Namah	Guru Of All The Worlds
75	Om Vyomakeshaya Namah	Whose Hair Spreads In The Sky
76	Om Mahasenajanakaya Namah	Father Of Kartikya
77	Om Charuvikramaya Namah	The Guardian Of Wandering Pilgrims
78	Om Rudraya Namah	The One Who Gets Sad By The Pain Of Devotees
79	Om Bhutapataye Namah	Lord Of Panchabhoota Or Bhootapreta
80	Om Sthanave Namah	Firm And Immovable Deity
81	Om Ahirbudhnyaya Namah	The One Who Possess Kundalini
82	Om Digambaraya Namah	The God Whose Robes Is The Cosmos

83	Om Ashtamurtaye Namah	Lord Who Has Eight Forms
84	Om Anekatmane Namah	The God Who Possess Many Forms
85	Om Satvikaya Namah	Lord Of Boundless Energy
86	Om Shuddhavigrahaya Namah	Lord Of Pure Soul
87	Om Shashvataya Namah	Lord Who Is Eternal And Endless
88	Om Khandaparashave Namah	Lord Who Wears Broken Axe
89	Om Ajaya Namah	The One Who Is Boundless
90	Om Pashavimochakaya Namah	Lord Who Releases All Fetters
91	Om Mridaya Namah	The Lord Who Shows Only Mercy
92	Om Pashupataye Namah	Lord Of Animals
93	Om Devaya Namah	Lord Of Devas
94	Om Mahadevaya Namah	Greatest Of The Gods
95	Om Avyayaya Namah	The One Who Never Subject To Change
96	Om Haraye Namah	Same As Lord Vishnu

97	Om Bhaganetrabhide Namah	The Lord Who Damaged Bhaga's Eye
98	Om Avyaktaya Namah	Shiva Who Is Unseen
99	Om Dakshadhwaraharaya Namah	Destroyer Of Daksha's Conceited Sacrifice (Yagya)
100	Om Haraya Namah	The Lord Who Dissolves All Bondage And Sins
101	Om Pushadantabhide Namah	One Who Punished Pushan
102	Om Avyagraya Namah	Lord Who Is Steady And Unwavering
103	Om Sahasrakshaya Namah	One Who Has Limitless Forms
104	Om Sahasrapade Namah	The Lord Who Is Standing And Walking Everywhere
105	Om Apavargapradaya Namah	Lord Who Gives And Takes All Things
107	Om Tarakaya Namah	The Lord Who Is Great Liberator Of Mankind
108	Om Parameshwaraya Namah	The Great God

About Me

I am a lover of journeys, within and without. I'm a mystic poet who writes poems daily as part of my spiritual practice, and a featured writer of articles mostly themed on wellness. Writing is one of my most sacred ways of both trying to understand the world around me, and my own place in the world, and I write in many forms: poems, verse, short stories, short and long-form fiction and memoir. Whenever and however the words flow, I try to let them! But flow starts with the body, without which we couldn't do anything at all. I'm a certified yoga teacher and Reiki master and I love taking long walks with no destination at all, bare feet when I can. My coaching services include story consulting and editing, and using meditation, yoga, journaling and other forms of creative expression as a path toward healing, growth and empowerment. When I'm not communing with trees, dreaming of beautiful tomorrows, taking photographs or sewing cloth paintings, I am back again with words, working on a memoir and a novel. My published poetry collections are *Formation: Along the Ganges and Back Again* (2015), *Little Poems for Big Seasons* (2016), and *Land* (2018).

I'd love to hear from you! Connect with me here:

Instagram: @tammystonetakahashi
Website: www.tammystone.weebly.com

Printed in Great Britain
by Amazon

32156731R00103